LITTLE MYTHS

LITTLE MYTHS

beth woodcome platow

The National Poetry Review Press

Warrenton, Oregon

The National Poetry Review Press
(an imprint of DHP)
Post Office Box 670, Warrenton, Oregon 97146

Printed in the United States of America
Published in 2017 by The National Poetry Review Press

ISBN 978-1-935716-42-6

For My Mother

CONTENTS

I.

I did everything to find you/
You run and hide/
I run behind you/
I run behind you/

Daniel Ahearn

Fiction

We all go untouched, is a lie.

We think in heavy thoughts, is a lie,

is a bed, is a thing we all need in the heat.

Somewhere the centuries

are building up like a brothel queue.

No better time to tilt your head back.

We all know how, is a lie.

The bed, like a gorge, is a lie.

I want to say *it's me*, where you are.

What you're touching with your hands is, too.

Non-Fiction

And you altered things about yourself.

Is that a question or an answer?
When I was born, it was known that I would
have to lie in order to live. Even swaddled,
we're all little myths waiting to unfold.

My father ate my mother,
my sister married my brother,
the gods weren't merciful.
Behind that, in the curtains,
I concocted myself out of the scraps.

This my memory; this is what it had to be
in order to survive.
I think we alter according to necessity, and
the truth is what we're willing to die with.

Did you cling to that image
because that's how you wanted to see yourself?

Ouch. I see myself as you see me
because I'm young.
There are at least ten wars
right behind your back,
but all you can do is look at me.

If I perjured myself, it's not
that I truly knew I had. I swear it.

The definitions are confusing.
All I know is that I held myself up
against the light, and a real image came through.

Mistress

If I come close,
and lie two shy lips.

If I press,
mark and animal you.

If I pretend you, no
daughters and no wife.

If I red prayer book,
if I church. Forgiveness,

come home.
I'm only good,

my body has crime.
If I, with wish

take you there, your hands.
If I circle you, what will.

When Even You Will Be Quiet

Let's meet at the gothic hotel,
the one that shivers.
The door unlocked for both of us,
as we arrive separately, and dirty.
Meet by the radiator that spits water
at our ankles so as to say:
let this room be flooded.

We're thin again. Leaning back,
my body heating
the frozen wallpaper, moistened
onto older paper by maids many years ago.
A tradition of sticking.

Outside the long windows is another country
where bells endlessly search for each other.
This, dear, is the easiest city
in which to stop suffering.
This is the place
in which the town hall is always closed.

Today, pomegranates have stained
my teeth a small murder.

Outside, the riotous are missing.
You're not noticing the odd lack
of shrieks. Have we come to the wrong city?
The air is light red. They have this address,
so we must leave the shower running.

I cross the room to the balcony.
My skirt sounds like flames rising
to the fifth floor of a brick building.
I look back and you notice my hair
says all the things I had wanted to.

For days we could stay here,
as each hour you take our temperature.
We can rest our heads. We can burn.

Aubade

On little slips of paper
passed under the door,
each hour, the owner has asked us
to leave. After the tenth I believe it:
the world has decided to approach.
I reach out for your arm, but you can't.

It's hard to distinguish morning,
except for the constant
clinking of milk bottles
that I've come to understand
as a procession of boredom.
Men in white suits, with paper hats,
secretly wishing for the cream
on their fingers. It's been years
since they've had the pleasure of glass,
of delivery.

It's as if a regime has ended,
but we didn't get the news of its start.
I wonder how, for whose sake, we
ignored the whispers in the room
that were not yours, and were not mine.
There seemed no way of remembering
that in the morning you'd need
to be returned.

Departure

We hurry to pack, aware
That far away, someone
Is trying to starve us.

Let's be honest,
Carry our little altars
In our arms and go home
To our families to say:
Two, and you are not one of them.

Who can know how
I ever made it to you.

A boat meets us on the bank
And as we head down river,
Behind us our hotel is glowing,
Conceiving. Two, like no
Acquaintance you've ever made.

I don't know who we are, but
Two, and the records are growing.
Two, and I'm not lying.

Decadence

The town's whispers
are turning red and the voices,
like a barn fire, get the horses panicking.
The window panes of these quarters belong
to neither of us, and they chatter
all night long.

When I choose to,
I can recall all the days I've ever lived.

Pulling back the curtain,
I understand where I am.
I understand why we celebrate
the seclusion of being partly wanted.
How thankful can I be? And who will answer?
You say my name,
lead me by my largest disaster,
and have me be quiet.
I don't respond to much anymore.

If I were to turn to you in my sleep
and show you my face
you would know that I dream
of your wife and daughters.
Their mouths are filling with grass
as the fields are spreading.
Let me assure you they're so pale,
and can't wake up.

Redemption Rock Road

The white sky, like the inside of a sick
mouth, has arrived. A car rolls by,
almost too delicate to be
a machine. We hold so tight
to each other, as if falling off.
Everything is against us,
we know this.

My daughters and wife are at home.
I imagine them swaddled
in a cocoon that I've had to build.
Their eyes peek out,
dead berries. It's easier
to leave them this way.

There is a road I take
between my homes
that dares me to understand
what I do. There are two stop signs,
a silo, and a stream that runs
along this road. Sometimes
these are the only things
I want to know.

You Are Going into a Quiet Despair

Remember I designed an escape route.
Remember how I lived once,
on a roof above all the doors.
If you leave I promise sadness.

But come with me to the edge
of the room, the place you avoid
for its infidelity. Listen,
there are so many places to go.

Let me rub your back, my doe,
this is life. The knocking in the pipes
and the image of someone, possibly me,
walking backwards.

Postcard

This morning the three dogs shat
on the floor and that's what I woke to.

Before I even woke my body took them
in, took them in like a mother would.

Not every mother, but let's get back to you.
One dog is now sleeping at my feet.

I know how that feels, that shame.
This is my sixty-seventh postcard.

Each time, when I say
I wish you were here

I mean to say *stay home,*
it's already over, I can't forgive you.

Joan of Arc Before Burning

Above all things:
God.

My skin is at risk.
Rope to neck.
Rope to wrist.

Please don't touch me anymore, but if you do
Don't call it *touching*.

Leave me
Without exits.
I know God understands this need.

I admit
All the fingers of my hands are not sinless,
But they are only my body.

#999, Red

Not a color, but something
that happened.

Like the year the bed
was shared and you forgot

everything that happened
at its edges.

Not shared, but emptied.
Not emptied, but utterly.

I wrote it all down while you slept,
and I did not ever.

Not a color,
but a reflection of what you've done.

Not a mouth,
but a place to be hurt and by this I mean:

an adult orphanage.
At best, another *if, then.*

A thing smeared,
and not even that.

Traveling

This ache is a bad girl.
This ache leads to a private suitcase

full of red fruits set down at the feet.
I have so little to offer

that you could understand,
that you could actually devour.

Do you know that impulse?
To eat until you are ready to love.

To love until you are going to die.
We call it gluttony.

In the end there's nowhere to move
other than towards you

which is to say:
Full. Stand. Still.

Taken

What I take from your throat
could save me. I imagine

this is happening
because if I am almost

gone then there is space
to notice me. *Pay attention*

to me. I'm nearly
the highest point in the city.

I can hear the sounds of my body
younger than I am now.

I was an ache
before I was anything.

Mostly what this sounds like
is necessary rummaging,

like a small animal searching
for something smaller,

something that wants to be taken,
and almost knows it.

Veronese

Finally, I am past all vehicles,
beyond all the rain in my hair.

It's crazy kind of weather here.
When I get to you, you're freckled

everywhere I'm allowed. I can't think
of what to do with a fork, with the wet basil

in your garden. When I'm lost, I'm always
contagious and slightly hungry. Give me

something strong, both plagued houses.
Give me some reason for a dagger, or poison

or even Verona. I'm dizzy and we haven't
even moved yet. We hum anemic funerary songs

after a full day of longing for white sheets.
We spend hours only touching inner arms.

This is How I Celebrate
Another Year of Red Leaves

Today my hair, my own russet field,
was caught on a bedpost. Each day is filled
with odd occasions. I like the fat girl
whose eyes bulge from just sitting.

The silos are full and we've no intention
of sharing. I've been churning butter
for at least seven thousand days
and it's never been tasted.
Today is a decision I keep

coming back to. It sits outside my room
with the simple smell of tea
and various unheard stories of hearing loss.
The sunrise is always the same
temperature here, and my heart—

its coma has nearly outlasted
every season of kale.
A mosquito takes blood from my neck
and all I can think of are men's hands
digging out turnips, working.

What I Know in the Dark

As if I were proper and kilted,
every touch comes secretly with me.
My fingers slipped along your back.
My picket fence, you.

I know, they've been predicting humidity
here for centuries. There's a lack
of breathing in New England

and you won't sleep any blue
when you do, finally, sleep.
The garden is quiet and has stopped
taking water.

I know why you love in swarms,
by months. I know you're like me at night:
astir, aching, simple.

There Was No Way of Getting Back

I can hear the seabirds circling our roof,
they've come inland to be hungry.

I want what a bird wants:
flight, a small life, to smooth midnight.

I want to feel faint.
Of course it's Sunday

and everyone seems to have neglected
their hanging gardens.

The store is out of gauze and aspirin.
This week two girls decided simply

not to be alive. But you swear you heard
intricate cello music coming from between

someone's legs on Redstone Hill.
This is a town that is swollen

and has hollows. I have no recollection
of these woods, of the peat and lovemaking,

of where to put your mouth
while we are here.

Sterling Junction, Centuries Ago

A little town has crept into me—
a sunken textile mill, orchard sighs,
a petticoat tossed in the reeds
by Lake Waushacum.
Tomorrow I'll bring you pears, my hands,
whatever you need. My mother says
farmers keep dying from their wives.
I've requested milk
and blankets from the neighbors.
I'm waiting for word. It's sour here.
Everything is hotter than my mouth
and the night is sick
with mustard clouds.
You said there were animals to tend to.
I'd loved your acres,
your weakness for this place.
So, I sit back, bear more life,
call this one bruised.

The Town

It's hard to separate life
from one's own version of it.
For instance, *I died.*
In actuality, *I'm still alive.*

Don't you see that junction ahead,
Routes 12 & 62
where all of the local urges meet,
where you go

to hold a town meeting
to request documentation
of the conception, delivery,
and burial?

It's impossible to prove you weren't
an auburn horse.
One thing to agree upon
is the smell of wool in rain,

and that is as universal as we can be
given our history.
If you say it's summer,
at least say it's winter, too.

There are half of us who grieve
the overuse of light,
who take the new weather
as a personal ache and tax.

Townspeople!
I don't say this to hurt you;
If I wanted to hurt you
I'd say something different.

It's delicate work explaining the story
of one town, one collective
divided and sub-divided
like the body of a discounted lamb.

Where Did My Body Go When It Went

The bed is the last place I remember it,
not sleeping
but it was there thinking:
I'm losing.

Thinking:
How is it I'm never perfect?

My body pulled itself
against the night. That place!
The simplest place to be
cross and alone.

Thinking:
I'm older than I should be.

What I believe happened is that
it fell away from itself.
The hours were so serious
and no one came.

Sweden

Try hard, it's midsummer.
You're a little ill, these waves.
You're a little gone. Sailing on the Baltic,
with a man, while your mother's dying
at home. Remember that. Her dying
is all over the place. It followed you,
little bug. Your grandmother called,
your mother is dying, only louder:
your mother is dying! You're missing it.
What kind of kind are you?

Today, my God, the smothered
herring, I ate so many things.
Don't touch. Not like that, or now.
You feel life scared to live itself.
You're north, with this failure.
Here, this land of bereaved nights
where the sun hangs its own
noose and won't climb in.
What have you gone and done?

Little Gun

A persuasion of doctors
comes by with a white glow
that even I cannot match.

Their coats are brighter
than my army of cells.
Left, right, left.

My skin, an operation itself,
has begun to grow back
as a layer of my new life in frenzy.

What I feel, I feel so strangely.
What I hear are glass noises
I can't preserve.

Someone is trying to speak
to someone I'm not,
and that hurts my heart.

I want to live again with my body
closed. I want to know my own mind,
my little gun,

is different from the morphine
that is pumped into my room
each day.

Hometown

The shame in the church
crawls out of each human.
A mild sin grows first
behind the ears.

The wind: it comes without thought
or any use of my hands. My hair
grows the same color as the red scarf
covering a lamp. I've heard of women
who lead men into a chamber
that is stained like the pit of a cherry.
Place something upon the tongue.
Go in peace.

Pretending there's no time to stop
and look at the old gravestones
that lean south, my father keeps driving.
The common is cold and blown clear
of leaves. This is near Chocksett School
playground where a German shepherd
tore up my soft back.
My father took me to the dog
that night to let it smell me.
I held it in my arms.
We're all bound to something.

The strain of the body in trauma stresses
the heart muscle. When I come up for air,
the wind fills my throat

before I realize I want it to.

When I think of what I am,
think of this small town.
The dog, my back, the women, my dog.

Leaving Season

In the fields, we've only just heard of love.
Everyone has this sort of life, don't they?

My sister and I learned the color of cornstalks and illness.
There were bad girls husking along Route 110.

You would tell us you might send us there.
You lined us up with sad pumpkins and the insane.

Somehow, through the same daily recollection
my sister and I are always delicate and fatherless.

We are thankful for the grass that is made for cows,
for tiny noises, for crouching by electric fences.

My sister and I have heard that there is an end to America.
We believe in rental cars and regeneration.

Now we go south. The clouds collapse here,
and strange how they look like we did.

We travel through groves of orange. We hear cicadas
molting. They never have to go back.

The long grasses and the wind.

I can't tell you how much.

The day is sore,

one long boundary.

This is my life,

this is yours.

I'm on the steps to the house, begging.

The first time I've had to.

What will happen without you?

Click of neighbors' sprinklers, the sun.

I hate this. Picket fence,

no voice, vacant house.

The Greatest

My grandfather lost his eye
and let it go a bluewhite/ A pipe
had dropped and cut it while he was
looking up/ trying to stop a leak/
or maybe he was looking at the sky
through a telescope/ as Americans do/
thinking the moon is our own/ Maybe
his eye saw something before his brain
could/ and that was it/ I don't know
what/ our government is doing up there/
but I know astronauts come back/
and don't come back/ I know he was
a patriotic man/ too/

My grandfather died on the other side/
of a boxing match/ He weaved in and out/
of a place or a feeling/ that I couldn't get
to/ His opponent pulled him into his chest/
the way fighters often do/
when they're tired/
It looks so much like love/
but it's brutal/

My grandfather never went to church/
while I knew him/ but there we sat
in the pews/ and sometimes
down on our knees/ I tried
to imagine his milky eye/ now boxed
with his body that had travelled

to war and back/
both the place and the feeling/
But he didn't die
that way/ in the South Pacific/
with the moon shining
off the barrels of guns/ He died
an old man in a bed/ in his house
with all the versions of himself pleading/
for the final bell/ Of all the deaths
he had/ this one hurt him
no more or less/
but it nearly killed us/
his fans/ family

The Long Field

There are some things we remember identically.
For example: when I was a child,
I wasn't a child.

My memory is like a bird placed in a box
and put into a long field.
It suffered and was softer for it.
When I say *suffered*, I mean *caught*.
When I say *caught*, I mean *born*.
When I say *born*, I never mean *died*.
Stay with me: I'm an optimist now.

Stay with me: It wasn't a bird and it wasn't a field.
We were fishing, alone.
That's when silence was like three rocks.
Spilling from one of my hands to the other for hours.
Silence: Something returning
again and again.
You must have touched my head,
or at least my shoulder.
You stayed with me.

The Barn

I would put you in a barn, alone,
not even the animals would stay
with you. No hay to sleep on
or braid into your hair. No
woolen horse blanket or smell
of leather tack. Just muck,
the possibility of fire,
and a jammed door.
I would bring you water,
once a day, show you
my face in which you would search
for your own. Stones
would replace my heart
for a short time as I slipped
by you, pitcher in hand.
Guilt is a forager and will find you.
Maybe I would help you drink,
or place the water out of reach.
I know I wouldn't sing to you,
in any language, even one that angered you.
It hurts the most to be given silence,
rather than choose it.
I know. I hurt someone.
This was my barn, once.

The Door

When you come to a door
do not think you need to open it.
When the door is a man,
close it. When the door is a man
rub your body against it.
When the door is a woman
smooth your hair.
When the door is a woman
kneading dough,
ask if you can help.

When the door revolves
do not get your hand caught.
Remember some people
lose a hand for simply touching
in certain parts of the world.
But in your world, where your door
swings its mouth open
and closed, don't be the servant
between kitchen and dining.
When the door is rich
and sunned and toned
don't avert your eyes.
Remember where you come from
is a beautiful fact.

When it's a fire door,
trust there's an alarm
because there will be a fire.

If the door is hot to the pads
of your fingers, try the escape.
Let the windows be the door.
But when *you* are the door,
like an army of doors,
like dominos lined up
waiting to be set into motion,
forget what I first told you.
Sometimes you need to open it.

II.

I will only call for you so long/
You may never come to me/
You may never come to me/
Come on, come on/

If you can't pull through/
there are things I can do/
and things I won't do/
Come on/

Annie Lynch

Marriage, East Berlin

I.

It came in like a quiet boat at night.
We still don't know who sent it
or why. Some days it makes us shake.

We kept on cooking for each other
and bathing ourselves.
We looked at children
but the sound of Chopin
always replaced the sight of them.

In its coming, it took away.
Over the years we grew
to understand that we were losing
our hold on each other
even though at night we would
send the gift of one thought
back and forth,
I'm here if you need me—

Back and forth,
in our sleep.

I'm here even if you don't.

II.

When the wall came down
we went in the other direction.

It was not freedom we wanted,
but to be tied forever to a man
in a room, through a wiretap,
listening to the sound of our breathing
and reporting back to his superior
that we ached for basic things:
our fathers, a baby,
and a way to understand
how to exit this life
without each other.

When we lost you we didn't know
if you chose another world, another place
nestled in the belly of another animal.
We didn't know if you felt that feeling:
Let me live, let me live some more!
How do you feel that feeling, being so small?
How do we feel that today, or tomorrow,
or next November? Do we feel it
with our hands, the soft skin of our toes?
Most days I forget I have these things.

.

Easter happened, just like that.
Who said we were ready for it?
You were gone. Little embryo.
Your ears not even fully formed,
which seemed the most unfair.
What appeared most divine that day
was the boat we saw, on the river,
stuck on a rock. That, we understood.

.

A healer came, swept me with her eyes,
and told me that I should sleep cold
and wake up warm. She put pins in my body,
the smallest knives, but it didn't hurt!
Oh, you! Are you thinking of me now,

as you begin somewhere else?
Will I always be your mother?
I wake up in the mornings freezing.
I stand up from the bed like a Soviet statue
and wait all day for spring to come back.

A Little Death in the World

I.
We found traces of the beginning.
You know what I mean.

If you don't know what I mean, you will.
Your truth is only as real as mine is.

II.
It was a fact, and not a feeling:
Water, life, and a thrump.

Can we prove happiness? I saw your note,
In the margins, that maybe there is a God.

III.
Then it was gone,
And we could not measure
The distance or the volume
Of that particular loss.

If there were ever a truth, it would be this:
We don't want to be crazy anymore.

We don't have the heart for physics.
If it was here, then bring it back.

The New Life

We wiped it down, measured it,
and bought stocks for it.

Someday we'll tell the story
of how it was born during several wars
that we were able to ignore.
We'll take it to Sachsenhausen
and show it all the shoes
and the things we're capable of doing.

In private we cried for all the pain
it took to get it, hold it, worry for it.
We took it home, introduced it to milk,
air, and television.

One night, while we had heat,
and food, and freedom
I looked behind me, bent down,
and whispered to it:
I need to die before you do.

Bekommen

In your father's language
a baby is *received*, not *had*,
in which case: we got you.
Because your heart
is a horse race
that a whole country watches,
mint juleps in hand.
Because you can't
often look us in the eyes
you are
like all the other
animals who know.
Because it seems impossible
that we created you,
but rather you arrived,
tornadic with emotion
that you brought
from other centuries—
prehistoric debris
we can only see
in the back of your eyes
with a flashlight
while I hold your hand
and let the doctors
try to understand you.
You came to us
wild and stunning.
Not one horse,
but one hundred.

Mid-Summer

You sit stemming strawberries and waiting
for an emergency like cancer
or a scratched knee. A phone call
is ringing through the body at all times.

You hire a lawyer
who only accepts money
and a glass of water to create
a Last Testament and Will
before a flight. The ashes, if a body
is recovered, should be buried
at Walden Pond where you bathed once
after a man in a bed in Cambridge
held your throat too tightly
and you tried to consider
if that was affection
while a train slammed by the windows
like it also slams by the pond
headed to Fitchburg, like Thoreau
described, that city where you were born
up a hill, in a storm to unhappy parents,
not because of you but just *unhappy*
the way adults can be.

You've never understood why they put a train
there even though you understand greed.
You wonder who makes these decisions.
You decide you have very little to give
so you leave your diamond ring
you rarely wear to your daughter

so that if your husband remarries
he won't be able to give it to another.
There is always one question:
How is this happening?

All of this from a tall, optimistic day
mid-way through this allotment
we call life, while your little girl's hair
moving through air
in the back yard seems to conduct
electricity through every wire,
in every place, reaching every hospital's
machines that are supporting life,
pumping morphine, restarting hearts.

The thought of losing her or him
makes you nick your thumb
with the paring knife
so you suck at the blood
with your mouth that has been working
since that very first day up the hill,
in a mill town called Fitchburg.

Mooring

You'll come to learn that my father left

when I was a child & your father's father

died in a Berlin prison. We exchanged

these stories the night we met

like vows that had already married us.

Now you're the child. We look at you & think

you're going to run off the dock.

At age three you move so hard

we imagine your body

won't contain you for much longer.

Twice a fire followed us. My building burned

the skin of the city one night,

like the boiling milk that spilled

on your father's arm when he was your age.

These were the gifts we brought

to the wedding.

Sometimes we pause & we panic.

We look for ways to anchor everything.

Before we lose you we anticipate losing you,

stare at you when you sleep wondering

who you will take & who you will take after.

Sick Day

When I called out from work
I said it was because_____was sick.
She wasn't sick but she died in my dream
the night before. In a dream no one records
the time of death. No one prepares.
No one goes to bed thinking:
When I wake up I'll be ruined.
I'll know what it's like to lose a _____.
But who can know what this is like.
Can those who live it know,
and can we call that living?
When I woke up, I couldn't.

I lay in bed with _____ all morning,
attentive in a way I'm usually not.
Even her hair was alive. Her heart
was moving like a soft machine.
She had no knowledge of her own passing.
I kept my face to the side of her face.
If you go, I'm coming with you.

Somehow the day had a place to be,
but I couldn't move or let _____ move.
If it happened once, like the longest length
of any night, like a hand grabbing
the contents of that night, it could happen
again. If time happens, if harvest happens,
if even once a soldier died. If some one,
then every one. I can't even name her.
I'm scared I said she was sick.

Gravity

If I am to pour myself out,
pain by pain, I know the source starts
higher up than any man
has ever been, in layers above the earth,
far above the blue halo where
wave-lengths scatter a cushion
of the best light around our planet.
Underneath clouds mass like targets,
bearing down.

That's where I live. Some days I stand
outside and wait for more or less
feeling, but it is always more,
sometimes in the form of rain
but also sun after the clearing
which is never a clearing, for me,
since I brought her into this world.
My child came from those layers.

My fear is the shape of an almond.
It stores itself in the center of my brain
and slowly petrifies me. Soon I will be rock,
a collection of weight, provenance unknown.
Someone will look at my layers one day
and say: There is where she lived fearlessly
and there is where she changed,
crushed by a love that could not be fully
protected, sourced, or explained.

The Box

To us it's cardboard, but to you
it's the magic box, where you enter
as yourself and come out a car,
a pony, an Indian. We tell you
to say Native American, because it's right
to say that now, except for Jill
who studied Indian law.
I know, sweetheart, it's confusing.
You are three right now and things are not
as they seem. You're three right now,
you see a picture of female anatomy
at the doctor's and you ask if you, too,
have little fists inside of you.
You do, you do.

You have a history I'm scared to tell you,
and not only your German side.
For that we'll visit Bergen-Belsen
and Buchenwald, and we'll quietly notice
the quiet, the impulse to say I'm sorry
to the empty space, to try to exist
without shame in the center of our shame.
Your eyes are very blue.

All the while I'll whisper in your ear:
You're good, you're good.

But you need to know that you are
also *possible.* Inside you
there is a darkness that we'll need to manage.

I'm not scared of you. I'm scared of us.

We have a photo on the wall,
of your great-grandfather walking
with Martin Luther King, Jr.
You look at it sometimes.
Right now you're three,
so he's just another man, with a tie.
We don't know the day, but it will come
when we tell you this history.
The history of skin. The history of ships.
The history of taking other people's things.
By things we mean:
names, land, bodies, children.

You go inside your magic box
and you come out a wolf,
wolf, wolf, wolf, wolf, wolf.
If you say it long enough
it will lose its meaning,
and we wonder if it's always a wolf.

The Cave

He & he & he & he left me,
& once that leaving got flung out
there was no stopping it.
It cycled into traffic, got hit,
& toppled over a windshield.
It landed on the street on its back.
A ragdoll, it stood up, gained balance,
& got back on its bike.
The car that hit it sped off.
Then people watched the leaving leave,
again, pedal furiously to its cave.
That's where the leaving go,
even when they're struck.
An ambulance came & drove around
the same square twice.
People pointed to where the leaving crashed,
only wind as proof of the accident.
But it wasn't an accident.
I think of the crash when I ride my bike.
Even when I ride slowly and with joy,
even with my daughter lodged
in the back bike seat, her hands
tapping my jacket as the wind says yes
to both of us. Even when I'm like that,
the leaving feels chemical,
lodged in my brain like a quiet firecracker.
Slow explosions feel like the accident
again, working hard against this new life
I've built.

Mother Life

A life has stretched this far,

tired & climbing forward

if only for the child

in the next room, who is singing

to herself because she is a child,

un-tired, only growing more

silken hair, more urgent in her beauty.

In this quiver of air that moves

between myself & myself,

I sometimes embarrass the adult

I've become. I'm older.

I've eaten too much.

I have lived in this distance too long,

so far away from myself.

My daughter one room over puts her lips

together attempting to whistle

& runs to find the person who can teach her.

She disturbs the space that is emptying me,

pulls at my body until I reach her

space which is kind & electric.

She reaches for the air of my whistle,

& says, *perfect.*

My Own Tonnage

I will tell you the story without telling
the story.
There's a door, a Dutch door,
a double door.
There's a weight not unlike pressure
or measure.
A boat not like a carving
but like a whale.
Not a killer, but almost,
as my body.

There are things that are and that aren't.
There is pain and there is more,
not unending but nearly.
Of course there are bees
but there might not be soon.
There is forbidden and there is verboten.
There is not enough language
to serve a craving.
There is America and not America.

You don't see pies cooling
on a sill but you did once,
so imagine that when you see
a storage of guns
or a man yelling dirt
from his swastika mouth.
If you inherit my gene
you'll want to hold him

by the shoulders and root around
his eyes to find
the moment he wasn't like this.
There, there it is.
He's small, watching ants in the dirt
under a lemon tree.
And maybe all the time before.
I hear you saying,
Turn the page, see what happens!

There are men and there are more men.
They will never not be.
A father, a son, a brother, a plumber,
a lover biting at your lip
like a last meal.
When there is loss hold its face
in your hands. Remember
it is every person, good and bad,
that has ever been.
Imagine the pie, maybe berry.
Imagine the lemon tree hosting a fly
who does not feel this life
like we do
except for the pleasure
of stopping, landing, dragging its legs
through the sugar.
Sugar that is the story which ends with you,
my own tonnage.
There's a daughter here now.

Acknowledgements

"The Box" was published in *Harvard Review*

"The New Life" and "A Little Death in the World" were published in *AGNI* Online

"Hometown" and "Marriage, East Berlin" were published in *Ploughshares*

"When Even You Will Be Quiet" was published in *Gulf Coast*

"Sweden" and "Decadence" were published in *Columbia Journal of Art and Literature*

"This is How I Celebrate Another Year of Red Leaves" was published in *Born Magazine*

"Leaving Season" and "Sterling Junction" were published in *Del Sol Review*

"There Was No Way of Getting Back" was published in *can we have our ball back*

"The Long Field" and "Non-Fiction" were published in *Redivider*

"The Town", "Postcard," and "#999 Red" were published in *Memorious*

"Mooring" and "The Door" were published in *Salamander*

"Sick Day" was published in Better

Notes

In the poem "Non-Fiction" the lines "And you altered things about yourself" and "Did you cling to that image because/that's how you wanted to see yourself?" are adapted from an Oprah Winfrey television interview with the author James Frey.

In the poem "You Are Going into a Quiet Despair" the general theme is taken from "The Man Who Walked Backwards" from the book *Parables of Kierkegaard*, edited by Thomas C. Oden, published in 1978 by Princeton University Press.

In the poem, "The Town," the line "I don't say this to hurt you; if I wanted/to hurt you I'd say something different" is from the poem "I Am Writing to You From a Far Off Place" by Henri Michaux.

The epigraph to part I is from Daniel Ahearn's song, "Don't Know What You Lost," from his EP *The End of Romance*.

The epigraph to part II is from Annie Lynch's song, "Come On," from the album *My Bonneville*, by Annie and the Beekeepers.

I'd like to thank the LeBlanc, Woodcome, Savage,

and Platow families, as well as the Bastling, Hehir,
O'Connell, Massouh, Fuoco, and Pinder families
for their guidance and generosity all these years. I
also need to thank the many people who helped
encourage, nurture, edit, proofread, and publish
these poems the past 20 years, especially my teachers:
Sue Rubenstein, Fred Marchant, Carol Dine, Lucie
Brock-Broido, Henri Cole, Ed Ochester, Karen
Volkman, Amy Gerstler, and Franz & Beth Wright.

The following people were among the many
friends who supported me and my work: Major
Jackson, Nick Flynn, Ilya Kaminsky, Carolina
Ebeid, Adam Dressler, Anna Ross, Steven Cramer,
Joan Houlihan, Kathy Nilsson, Jennifer Militello,
Daniel Ahearn, Rob Arnold, Melissa Chinchillo,
Tim Marten, Valerie Duff, Jim Behrle, Shannon
Gracia, John Mulroony, Clare Thompson, Victoria
Deischer, Alyson Campbell, Eric Drotch, Nils
Anderfelt, Chris Marstall, Elisa Ravella, Rachel
Redlener, Jill & Ryan Mastro, Christine & Ian
Stratton, Suzanne Cope, Doug Kohn, Deborah
Bennett, Anthony Scibilia, Kim Drain, Gail Vida
Hamburg, Vanina Marsot, and last but not least
the Potts Poets: Kirun Kapur, Mike Perrow, Brian
Burt, Amy Clark, Leslie Williams, Erin Trahan,
Kate Westhaver, and Lynne Potts.

I'd also like to thank Berklee College of Music's
departments of Faculty Development, Liberal
Arts, and Counseling & Advising.

Will, thank you for sitting on that couch, in that café, that amazing night. You changed my life.

Amelia, even in your youth you teach me more than all the poems ever have.